WHAT MAN IS THIS!

Poetry and Images Praising the
Power and Core Essence
of Ultimate Men
of Character!

by

winifred Mosetta hill

What Manner of Man is This!

© 2015 by Winifred Mosetta Hill

ISBN: 978-1-63110-188-5

All Rights Reserved Under
International and Pan-American Copyright Conventions.
No part of this book may be used or reproduced in any manner whatsoever without written permission except in the case of brief quotations embodied in critical articles or reviews.

Printed in the United States of America by
Mira Digital Publishing
Chesterfield, Missouri 63005

Dedicated

in memory of the Late

Winfred A. Scruggs

In Daddy's Care - Bayoc

and
in recognition of

Men

who are "Poetry in Motion" as

Achievers
Believers
Conquerors
Teachers

Coaches, Mentors, Providers, Leaders

Credits

Artists: Cbabi Bayoc (art prints framed)
　　　　Amina Terry
Photographers: Roy Robinson
　　　　　　　Richard Townsend – Now You See It Photography
Cover: Zs Layout Design
Images: community leaders, family, friends, TMC

"You are the salt of the earth; You are the light of the world…"

Matthew 5:13

Sharing your "ultimate" traits:
Your powerful **faith**
Your magnanimous **love**
Your approachable **meekness**
Your guiding **patience**
Your integral **righteousness**
Enhances our blessedness!

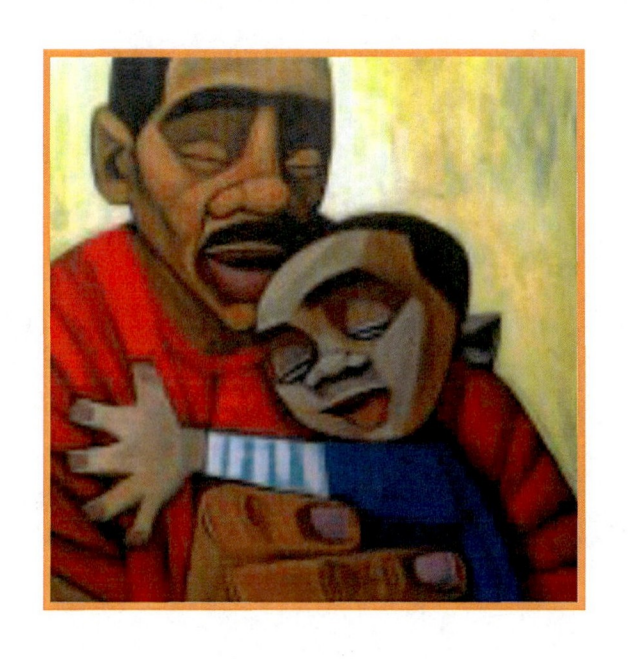

Great!
   Ultimate!
      Grand!

My Great Grandfather

by Kaleb

My great grandfather was truly great. He was a grand man. He taught his children a lot. He was a sharp dresser. He was sort of small but strong. He was also an artist. His name was Winfred Scruggs.

My great grandfather was so strong that he was a Concrete Finisher for a construction company. What did he do? He was one of the concrete finishers for the south entrance vertical sign at the St. Louis Zoo, the sign that spells ZOO. Also, on the exchange where Highway 70 goes over 270, my great grandfather helped finish the concrete on the bridge that runs 14 feet over the roadway. He made sure the express lane on Highway 70 was laid correctly. Also, he was a foundation repairer for under the McKinley Bridge.

My wonderful great grandfather laid the great foundation for my wonderful family.

He was the protector and provider for my grandmother's family.

My great grandfather was a brave, responsible, smart man.

WINFRED AREULIA SCRUGGS

Preface
Written with club members and restaurant guests

A MAN! AMEN

*He's a gentleman who may live on your street,
the polite righteous man women long to meet.
...for such a MAN let's say Amen!*

*He calls a female words that make her glow
not derogatory terms that cause her woe.
...for such a MAN let's clap our hands!*

*Consistent in keeping faith
Persistent in caring
Resistant in a mighty way
Resilient in sharing
Respectful
Protective and selective*

...for such a MAN let's say Amen!

*He makes a good friend, loving and kind;
Goal-oriented, with progress in mind.
...for such a MAN say Amen again!*

*Financially healthy, even if not wealthy;
He's stable and for that trait she's grateful.
...for such a MAN let's shout out Amen!*

... *for such a MAN let's say Amen!*

Consistent in keeping faith
Persistent in caring
Resistant in a mighty way
Resilient in sharing
Respectful
Protective and selective
. for such a MAN let's say Amen!

A MAN! AMEN

WELL, *COME*

WELCOME to this real man's house, where you never
    have to knock;
The entry is open, come on in, join His flock.
We offer you nourishment sent from above,
    encouragement, fellowship, and love.

Enter into this experience
    meant to uniquely bless your heart;
Enjoy the messages herein, about God's works of art.
He made you for His purposes, giving you the honor
    to do His will empowered.

Bring your need for betterment; our Savior is able.
    This heartfelt invitation
Is also a proclamation… a moment of appreciation
To celebrate <u>His</u> greatness in the fact of our creation*!*

Contents
(Unmasking **Ultimate Men**)

1. And ALL that Jass
2. Behold This MANner of Man
3. Best Dance
4. Big Daddy
5. Blessed and Assured
6. Boss up in Ones Face
7. Bossy is Costly
8. Brother-MaN
9. Brother-men
10. Champion
11. Charmer
12-13. Cheers*!*
14-15. Dad
16. Delightful Chosen Man
17. Endeared Endowment
18. Family Affair
19. Father
20. From Men to Boys
21. Get It Straight, Educate, Celebrate
22. God Don't Like Ugly
23. Greater is He
24. His Friendly Focus
25. His Friendship is a Kinship*!*

26.	His Hum-Along Song
27.	His Mind-Set
28.	His Vision is Wisdom
29.	Honoring Him Back in the Day
30.	HOPE Instruction
31.	Inclined as Designed
32.	Incredible Love
33.	Inspirer
34.	Just Because
35.	Kids to Ultimate Men
36-37.	Leading Man Attitude and Tools
38.	Man: A-1 Adept, Attuned, Amazing Achiever!
39.	Man Adorned in Majesty
40-41.	**MAN among Men** (Personalize this page)
42.	Man of Example
43.	Man Talk: Rejuvenation Revelation
44.	Man Talk: Witness to Goodness
45.	MAN: Tribute to Excellence
46.	MAN: Ultimate Runners for Justice
47.	Medicine Man's Prescription
48.	Mighty Man
49.	Mr. Fine
50.	New Position
51.	Nothing Between
52.	Permission
53.	Philosopher
54.	Pledge
55.	Positioned in Free Submission
56.	Positive Energy/Synergy
57.	Pretty Slick
58.	Prize Fighter
59.	Purposed in Progress
60.	Rare but Found

61.	Royalty Focus
62.	Success
63.	Stay Dressed Up
64.	Sugar Man
65.	Taught and Trained
66.	That Kind of Man
67.	Ultimate character Traits
68-69.	Ultimate MAN
70.	Virtual Reality
71.	Walking in the Valley
72.	Warrior Drum Major
73.	Watch Him Show, Tell, and Excel!
74.	'Way Up in His Sky / When? *Now! Win!*
75.	When She Whines
76.	Who is He? Power in the Crowd!
77.	Willing Winning Wise Worker
78.	Winning Wilderness Wars with Peace
79.	Wisely Abiding
80.	Words Smiling at Ultimate Men
81.	Workin' It With Him
82.	Yes, He is All That All That*!*
83.	You Know What?
84.	You're Steppin
85.	You've Surfaced in God's Love
86-87.	Your Jazzy *JASS*
88.	ZONE: Business / Community/ Country
89.	ZONE: Family and Home
90-91.	ZONE: Teaching Hope and Victory*!*
92.	ZONE: Where Pride Resides
93.	ZONE: Dance Class
94.	ZONE: The Route Out
95.	ZONE: Training Space
96.	ZONE: MAN Hood

Back Cover: YOU Be an Author

Magnificent Mighty Men
    Contend bravely on to
        Face prayerfully up to
        Dancing on through the
Wilderness!

...And ALL that Jass
Resounding Profoundly
Moving us, shaking us with anointed ability
Moving us into an attitude of joyous harmony
Moving us into a progressive mood
       A partying interlude into our solitude
As smiling hearts relate with your smooth groove

Soothing us to
    Let a good time rule!
Resounding profoundly, your act is top class
Gospel-like rhythms in your genius jass
Your style sends a progressive mood
       Mellow tunes bringing plenty good news

Soothing us to
    Let the good times rule!
Messengers, playing encouraging inspiration!
Spreading caring in soul-stroking translations!
SENSATIONAL IMPROVISATION!

Music maker *making good times rule!*

1

Behold This MANner of Man

Magnificent, noble, total
Trustworthy and trusting
Bridge builder
Capable of sharing his realness
A private adventure into personhood
Controlling yet controlled

Highly esteemed
Richly redeemed
Able to *give* all if he wants to
Able to *take* all he wants, too
Able to lead – willing to follow
Gentleman
Whom she's glad to know
      Standing strong on his own
          Positively prone
              Born to win!

BEST DANCE!

Living the urge of manly dominance
    Dancing barefoot toward the promise,
Toes stepping out of hocus-pocus
    With free fun his only notion
A carefree competative beat repeats,
    Releasing eager feet
To skip to a galloping song;
    He joins the brotherly loud crowd
Growing in that free spirit zone
WHERE *BOYS WILL BE BOYS* with desire
To be faster, stronger, score higher,
Greeting each challenge *inspired!*

BIG-DADDY

Tastefully selective, he prepares a feast
To nourish with fruit from his family tree;
Big Daddy teaches **knowledge**
To flourish through good and bad times.
Mankind's revival is seeded and weeded
By wise decisions from "back in the day"
As he claims, *I know best, so do what I say!*

His soul strongly inclined and designed for victory
He clues kids in, to strength with strong beliefs
That incite doing well / Urging, go on*!* Now ***excel!***

Big-daddy! He dictates the menu…
Helps order priorities with healthy views;
Structures the future into positive venues
Teaching esteem and survival **rules**…
Thus the family circumstance includes
Plenty good news*!*

BLESSED and ASSURED

Authority kisses his forehead anointing his worth the moment of his birth.

Joy celebrates his curiosity for exploring, finding.
Hope dictates task completion, encouraging him to pursue paths of righteous positive decisions.

Patience helps him to envision big dreams and better conditions.
Wisdom prepares his table with healthy choices.

Integrity instructs him to obey the voice leading him to higher ground where pure waters shall bathe his soul in peace.

BOSS

He navigates the tasks it takes
Working to win first place
In the races on life's staircase

He decides what it takes
Steps up to the plate
Agrees to put what's needed at stake

He sets sight and demonstrates
The passion it takes to situate
Him in the goals he anticipates

Anxiously increases pace
Up in his face his boss says "wait"
(The verbal meaning of faith)
"Yes, you will hurdle obstacles,
As grace opens the gates,"

Mirrors the boss up in his face!

BOSSY is COSTLY

It costs to take a stand
Be strong as God's man
It costs to be your own b o s s
Regardless of others' demands
It costs to take the lead
Push ahead and succeed

It costs to set the pace
Smartly dressed to impress

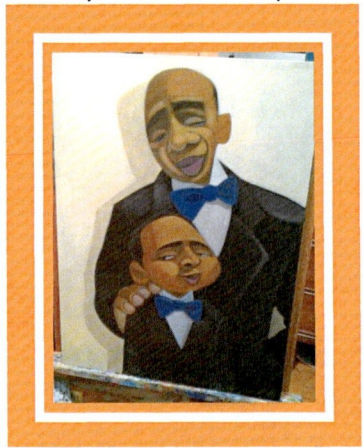

But it also pays

BRAVE MaN with Skills to Stand

Through storms leaning on his Savior's arm
Out-weathering much, he has come;
Determination uncompromised
Belief in self worth gives him pride.
He has thrived along highways and byways
Reducing trouble to nothing but an episode
Outside his abode;
Life may be cold but he knows his role;
"Ain't nobody's business but my own!"
        He walks tall through it all as God's man…

Attitude's in tact, to be exact, grace has his back;
For his work takes tough skills, little room for slack.

Responsible, he's supremely persuaded;
Thus the struggle has its rewards, and his debts get paid.

Moving on, his song is
"Ain't nobody's business but my own."
        He stands tall as God's man…

BROTHER-MEN

Rendering unto each other as brothers
    They reveal a plan
To foster high ideals among the young ones
With tough love enough to convince hope
To enter neighborhoods as we strive and cope.
    They reveal a plan
To lead the boys into brotherhood...
    They reveal a plan
To get them dressed for success...looking good
Doing the man-thing linking resources, assisting
Families in doing their business,
Growing boys into men...
    ...a victory plan

CHAMPION

Been treated unequally by the emotionally diseased,
He asserts his authority;
In ways that display he has come of age.

Transformation with constructive application
Of wisdom and vision in conversations
Grieves his enemies to devastation.

Sizing up others with mutual distrust
He makes waves and expects retaliation,
But also wins friendly spaces in alien places.

Realizing strength, says, "this too shall pass,"
As he gains esteem at an impasse to laugh
And sing a verse of "free at last*!*"

This far by toil, **prayer, and faith**
    Assured, having endured rugged days

Integrity Is his personal legend
As well as his powerful constant companion
    As life awards him the status of **champion*!***
"Champions aren't made in gyms. Champions are made from something they have deep inside them-a desire, a dream, a vision..." Muhammad Ali

CHARMER

We danced as you taught me new steps
Charmed me with your patience,
    "Step left...
        Step left... Now right;
            Now right;"
Grooving to soothing music,
Me, moving *left* as you said,

    "No, step right;"

We laughed as you led me with class;
Looked in my eyes, smiled and said,
"Darling, it's the best time I've had."
Your artistry
    And the music made me feel exceedingly
        glad, glad, glad...
    Charming me profoundly with your
        Jass.

CHEERS!

Cheers!
For YOU, Ideal Men
Who do not hesitate or wait too late...
Sedated at the gate...Too satisfied to anticipate
A state beyond our victimization
And to demonstrate authority... in the actualization
Of freedom from negative indoctrination
And to make the evaluation
That we are priceless humans
And union is good.

Cheers!
For YOU, Ideal Men
Who find ways to relate and negotiate
Beyond mistakes
And construct through caring collaboration
Changes with brotherly demonstration;
Men free from negative indoctrination
Who make the evaluation
That we are priceless humans

And union is good

Cheers!
For YOU, Ideal Man
Providing opportunities for others
Enrriching futures for sisters and brothers
For families, networking constructing pathways
Doing what it takes
Loving being essential
Rearranging, sustaining, training.

Cheers!
For YOU, Ideal Man
In the background being profound
Community is fortunate to have you around
Walk tall in mankind's hero parade;
We'll throw confetti along your way;
Big CHEERS!
Big CHEERS!

WHAT MANNER OF MAN! IS THIS!
The love of a man's heart,

DAD... a word of praise designed
In appreciation of dads throughout mankind;
    Especially to you who've been
A child's star hero and guiding friend.

    Great dads support kids to walk tall
And lift them up if they should fall;
    Great dads firmly push children on
Persistently until they've won.

    Great dads sometimes joke and play
But want kids saved, so often pray.
    Great dads teach right from wrong
And bring "consequence lessons" home.

A great dad takes a good stern look
At friends and reads them like a book.
    Your friends receive a frown or smile
A reminder: Respect his rules and child.

It's great to know a good true man
Who listens and then understands;
    Whose child securely believes,
Knows beyond doubt, "Dad loves me."

Childhood days, joyful and swift,
Bring memories, a blessed gift;
    For, love is part of a plan God had
In making a great man...calling him Dad.

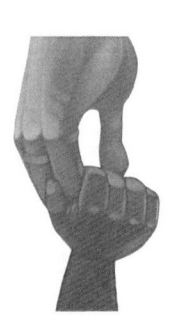

DELIGHTFUL CHOSEN MAN

Delightful confident man,
Her eyes consume
The elegantly groomed
Essence of your presence.

> Your manly grace
> Embraces her state
> Of mind to lovingly relate.

Her being is invited,
Desire ignited,
Uncontrollably excited,
To follow closely, holding tightly.

Uniquely you stand
Chosen, as you extend your hand
To your lady as her soulful total man.

Endowed ENDOWMENT Teachers

Sure, we've had
Dreary dark and stormy nights.
Perhaps some have been
Weary, nearly blinded in our plights.
BUT
He preaches and teaches that our
Survival instinct (obedience)
With FAITH
Takes us into a higher height...
With HOPE
Refuels us for a successful flight
    Into fullness of joy, to reach for our
Promised inalienable rights...
Directing a path with sunlight
Into an even better way to live life*!*

He reminds that Mercy
   Strengthens to hold tight and steadfast;
And that Grace
   Assures God's will that we be blessed.
> *"Thou wilt show me the path of life:*
> *In thy presence is **fullness of joy**..."*
> *Psalm 16:11*

FAMILY AFFAIR

Let our men commence as cousins
DNA blending us in as cousins
A living race of real cousins
    Who knows?

Let us be friendly cousins
Cousins who go around anticipating
Discovering even more precious cousins
    Who knows?

Let's party with cousins spreading hope
Shaking hands and greeting each other
Uniting us as sisters and brothers!

...Embracing each other as family
Growing strong roots from the family tree...
Ultimate men building a legacy
Of greatness as our ancestors dreamed
    Who knows?

FATHER

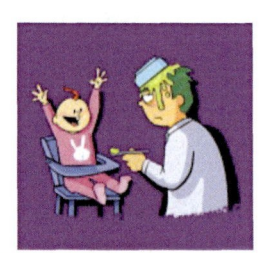

Father, we call you, worthy of all the name implies;
 Man of courage, encouraging family pride;

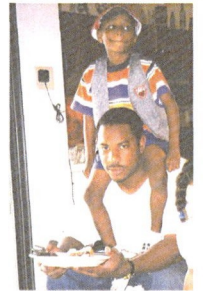

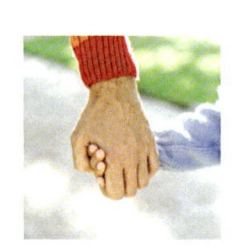

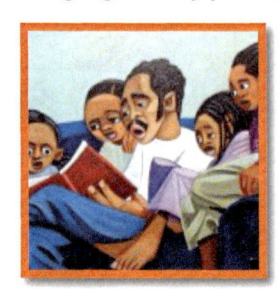

Impacting young lives;

A real Giant

19

FROM MEN to BOYS

Amid trespasses against them
Great men gather the boys
To hear new "do right" rap and songs
> ***Vocalizing lyrical spiritual ascent***
> ***Not vulgar lamented descent!***

...Telling how **foresight** must prevail
And **insight** must set their sails
Toward self-esteem and higher dreams.

Despite
Enemy plights and stormy nights
Their hopes must stay bright
Steering them right
> With fuel for flights
> Into *their* greatness.

...Standing tall
Even pulling up
Others who fall

GET IT STRAIGHT, Educate, CELEBRATE

Assignment: Explain the following.
*It's possible to receive the credentials you need to achieve what **you believe** you need to succeed.*

Reknown professsors profoundly agree:
    Listen well, let truth proclaim
    The lessons you need to gain;
Inch by inch
    Step by step
        Mile by mile,
Erase doubt…Just don't stop.
    Finding success is all about
        Closing gaps on the route.

Reknown professsors profoundly agree:
    You can do it if you wanna…
    But stuck in doubt,
    You're not gggggggonna!
Pray on!
    Pursue it!
        You can do it!

GOD DON'T LIKE UGLY

Now we do know God
Don't like ugly
Stuff like robbing and mugging.

And we know he don't like
Drug dealing and stealing
Somebody's life.

And we know he can expertly reveal
Disastrous reasons to heal
For the children's sake.

And we know he
Is greater than man
The gangsta and the klan
And has the upper hand
Regardless of their plans to end
The lives of black men*!*

Let the truth be boldly told
God don't like ugly
Regardless of the color.

GREATER is HE

He says
Greater is He that is within me
Than in all the world.

He lives
Emphatically for good.
Spiritual renewal improves

His voice to cheer
His soul to be free
His eyes to see
With integrity.

New reactions since his rebirth
Celebrate joy in self worth!

He stays loyal to a King
Greater than anything
Anything, everything.

HIS Friendly FOCUS

His focus is friendship given for free.
Friends are placed in a privileged category.
Also his focus is a new way to see
Visions of greater possibilities
Of how dreams can become realities

He and his **friends** claim a brighter destiny
New tools, new rules give them authority;
Not to mention thrilling self-esteem;
He out-distances resistance; now really free
New places, spaces, new heights he seeks

In rays of sunlight he can be seen
Dancing with brazen attitude;
In facilities requiring success abilities,
He enables joining in joy and harmony
Focusing with **friends** living life abundantly*!*

HIS FRIENDSHIP IS a KINSHIP!

He is proof of *truth* as an action verb
Transcending times past in memories...
Asserting trust highlighting discoveries
Big fun! You know such a special someone?
    Friendship is a sort of kinship
    With him, more than a relationship
    Extending reality into true caring...
    Replacing frowns with laughter
    Enhancing prime times sharing

This friend steps in as a situation regulator
    Shaking stuff down, turning strife around
    Spinning it into winning pound by pound
    To bake a better cake,
    Create a kinder place
Echoing "it's all good" with a tight grip
While cheering your dance at a faster clip...
That's a special kind of kinship**...**
Called ultimate friendship!

HIS HUM-ALONG Coping SONG

I'm so glad Jesus loves me
I'm so glad Jesus loves me
I'm so glad glad glad
Jesus loves me
So I repeat:
I'm so glad Jesus loves me
So I stand
    Loosen my fists
    Unclench my hands
    Proclaim again
I'm so glad
I'm so glad
So glad glad glad
Jesus loves me

HIS MIND-SET

He passes another stress test,
Gets up and shouts hooray!
Looks past strife sees hope and blessedness,
Glances ahead, grace says there's a brighter day;
It doesn't have to stay this way!
    Stands tall on his knees, prays
Lord, have mercy please.
Questions if he can reach the Promised Land;
Rubs his tummy; sin's menu looks yummy!
His world is in a whirl as he ponders,
    Am I still God's man?
    I **Am** still God's man...

Out of confusion
He draws a conclusion
To transition beyond fake ideals.
Recalls advice from his granny,
Smiles, hearing a solution to pursue
    Facts for living that old truths reveal...
Thinking, what's wrong with me?
    Temptation's got me greedily
Rocking in my soul...
Obedience is my role to gain control.
I'll win letting faith dictate my escape
Thus my *victory is foretold*...
    I am still God's **MAN**!

HIS VISION is WISDOM

He states
Envision how prayer will get you there
Envision how faith will open gates

He persuades
And demonstrates the way

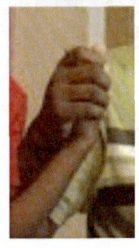

He praises
Prospering beyond common place
With applause for winning each race!

He celebrates
Family achievements made!

HONORING Him Back in the Day

Homemade aid from back-in-the-day,
Supplies proven solutions full of faith;
Homemade aid mixes time to pray
With hymns and fervent praise.

The formula from back-in-the-day
Insisted that children obey;
"Back talk" adults would not tolerate;
Respect and pride it tended to create.

Yesterday's menu has its merits;
Old school survival tools kids were learning
Godly guidance and ample supplies
Of spiritual fruit on which they thrived.

HOPE INSTRUCTIONS
from Pastors to Future Generations

In capital letters hear inside:
You are our source of P R I D E.
Strive bravely and be
WHO YOU WERE BORN TO BE.
keep HOPE

In capital letters hear it clear:
Our loving encouraging C H E E R S.
Disown fear,
Keep SUCCESS aims dear and near.
have FAITH

Capitalize on your reachable position,
    Arise into the promise
        Enjoying the ride
As you wisely arrive into whom
YOU WERE BORN TO BE*!*

INCLINED as GRACE has DESIGNED

WATCH As he pursues his needs

Grace strengthens him to proceed;
    Leads him and guides his feet
To press toward the mark on to victory*!*

SEE How when others say no
He smiles and finds fuel for the right way to go;
    Grace answers, "Follow, I'll show
Paths to where peaceful waters flow."

KNOW God's men are blessed with endurance
To complete a task or pursuance
    A voice of supreme assurance rings clear:
        "Do not fear, I am here."
Rooted in faith
Obedient in mind
Patiently paced

Successfully inclined*!*

INcredible LOVE

Love
Is but a word In case you haven't heard,
When it comes to comparing
With his / Which is
Uncountable bountiful treasure
Beyond any measure / Dependable, lasting
Incredible, in fact, fantastic.
Love
Is caring in action / A source of satisfaction
A circumstance beyond romance
That through true manhood lives
And gives such precious gifts.

Tribute: <u>Love's Character Revealed</u>
    Dear vessel of faithfulness
    Lovely garden of hope
    Deep resource of sunshine
    Prime example of "cope"
        Dear friend full of favors
        Loving and discrete
        You're dependable, discerning
        Strong and ruling but sweet*!*

INSPIRER

Precise and loud, distinctly speaking
because he wants us to hear

Succinctly, directly
because he wants to make it clear

Emphatically
With authority advises
And emphasizes each message
Not hinting or texting
Educating, illustrating
Unmistakably suggesting
What we may
or may not be expecting:

Dear Brothers and Sisters...
Listeners and resisters...
    ...end hesitating;
Keep CELEBRATING,
    With more praying,
    and praising;
Life is not playing
    ...Time is not waiting
Let's GET IT TOGETHER!
Let every soul be in subjection to the higher Powers...
Rom. 13:1-9

JUST BECAUSE

Our applause is
just because
You are
A righteous, delightful Man
Endowed with Vision, Wired with Wisdom

and just because
You are
A listener to a secret
With integrity to keep it
and just because
You are
A Mighty Man, fine reputation
Prayerfully oriented toward Rejuvenation
    Positive energizer
    Success inspirer
        Reality focused leader
        Gifted Teacher
and just because just because
You are that kind of Ultimate MAN

" ...for I am fearfully and wonderfully made..."
Psalms 139:14

KIDS and Ultimate MEN

KIDS *"Wrapped" in Ultimate Traits:*

Cooperation	in positive peer collaborations
Honesty	is my reputation
Hope	gives inspiration for my education
Kindness	to the population
Perseverance	is determination for my graduation
Respect	demonstration of my worthy station
Responsibility	is my obligation
	to plan my occupation
	in my own corporation

ULTIMATE MEN *"Rap" to* KIDS:

Cooperation	**with no hesitation**
Honesty	**is my verification**
Hope	**is my inspiration**
Kindness	**is my obligation**
Perseverance	**is my dedication**
Respect	**is my personal presentation**
Responsibility	**is my demonstration of self-preservation**

Leading Man Attitude and Tools

His authority is strength
Guiding our tasks to completion...
> **He gives much to his community.**

His joyfulness in caring
Helps heal and transform...
> **He gives much to his community.**

He manages projects and programs
For youth and seniors...
> **He gives much to his community.**

He researches opportunities to BUILD
  And politics to competently make hopes realities
He secures, and leads by notable deeds...
  He gives much to his community.

seventh consecutive year

topping the "most admired" list

"Care" Riders who send packages and support to troops and wounded warriors in various projects.

A-1 Man: Adept, Attuned, Amazing Achiever!

Ultimate Men,
Thank you for willingness to step beyond the call
To achieve, even exceed needs of betterment for all.
As examples of strength in overcoming situations
    As leaders with community and unity expectations
        As Ambassadors for youth and education
           As believers with prayerful dedication
                As warriors protected by our Lord and shepherd
                  As laborers toiling combining your efforts
                      As teachers anointed to speak with insight
                        As achievers giving back to reduce plight

As ultimate solvers of problems
As medicine men inventing healing solutions
As business men offering financial resolutions
As dissolvers of social toxins and pollutants
As contributors of time and donations for celebrations
As establishers of joyous family traditions and occasions…

Task completers upon whom we depend,
We salute you, Ultimate Men!

MAN Adorned in Majesty

Percy Pruitt, Author

Adorned for constant flight
Going through the vicissitudes of life
Having crawled
Through doubt, mistrust, and unbelief; 
Then
Robed in a cocoon of water,
Was transformed
Into a new creature,

Born again
    Adorned for God

MAN among Men

What's so grand about an **Ultimate Man**?
An adult male human who is and does this:

MANages to press through it all and stand tall
Mind of a giant to rise again if he should fall
MANages to break through if a crisis demands it
MANages to command if blocked in or stranded

MANages to make the odds work in his favor
Even convince teams to put forth the needed labor
Projects inspiration for mankind,
Courageously impacting future times.

MAN whose contributions will long remain
For he excels, builds, skillfully reigns.
MAN: A-1 Adept, Attuned, Amazing Achiever!
MAN among Men as follower and leader

Instills and applauds educational aspirations
MANages to reverse some adverse situations
Personifies courage as a victorious survivor
MANager of family as Provider and Supplier

Contender with an agenda to protect home
Defender with persistence to overcome
Gauges Satisfaction by Responsible actions
MANages to arrive and give others directions

Enjoins, assures, that youth can be heard.
Enjoys, endorses, employment of God's Word

Backbone...strong / Boldly faces-the music / Fortitude underscored / Gutsy / Lionhearted/ Reassuring / Valiant! *Motivational! Inspirational!* **SENSATIONAL!**

This name in tribute to an Ultimate Man's
essence of love   gentleness   goodness   faith   temperance:

_____!

Man of Example

Surpassing all the rest,
We observe him looking his best
Without even trying to impress.

Along with looking great,
He exhibits
Ultimate character traits!

MAN TALK: REJUVENATION REVELATION

God cannot fail so thru life's gales
He floats my boat and sets the sails
He lights the future to guide me through
Revealing his goodness like no other can do

Choir:
    Amen, Amen, say Amen*!*
Preacher:
    He Leads and teaches us how to stand*!*
People:
    Believe, receive, holding God's hand*!*
Choir:
    Amen, Amen, say Amen*!*

MAN TALK:
WITNESS to GOD'S GOODNESS

When you THANK him for his goodness
God reveals more blessings to you.
> *Team:* **Let's practice**

When you THANK him for his power
See how your life improves.
> *Team:* **Let's practice**

When you THANK him for his patience
He strengthens you with his grace.
> *Team:* **Let's practice**

Let us witness to his presence
Coming in 1st place *full of **noisy praise**.*
> *Team:* **Let's proceed**

MAN: Tribute to Excellence

We applaud him!
As role model awarding others' strengths;
Giving prime time, initiating events;
A man who puts in effort, planting seeds,
Citing individual and community deeds;
We pause to proclaim:
"What Manner of Man! is THIS!"

We celebrate him!
Foundation established for others' talents;
Supreme are his traits, kingly his essence;
We Salute His Excellence
Encouraging standards of achievement;
We pause to proclaim:
"What Manner of Man! is THIS!"

Man: Ultimate "RUNners for Justice"

reality paints a historical picture / ***run baby run***
runners pause before a memorial in the middle
of a street / and emotion overcomes
raising awareness of a tragedy / **20** days of running
raising awareness of a tragedy/ **540** miles of running
through elements determined to show
hope against injustice, for brutality has exposed
      THEY have a reason to run / A reason to run
Run, rather than succumb to mind incarceration
Run to raise awareness of violent life-ending situations
Run towards the problem
Robed; clothed in mind emblazoned with the phrase
    "Run for Justice"
Not an aspiring political proposition
But a plea against unjust conditions
    20 days of running*!*
        540 miles of running*!*
           35 miles a day running*!*
Racing against the grain / For nothing?
History pictures it plain
Justice is insane / Society is to blame
    Running, victory to claim
    Running towards an elusive equality dream
HE kneels in the street engaged in an evasive scheme
Rises to run again / Contends till with prayer ascends
As a man **empowered to win***!*

In recognition of Londrelle Hall and Ray Mills

MEDICINE MAN'S PRESCRIPTION

Eradicate
>Wipe out the post-slavery syndrome
>Of self-hatred started
>>when stolen from home

Refute
>The abusive funk-tioning in songs
>Let the healing come
>>declare the feelings gone

Rebuke
>The spirit of doing each other wrong
>Let the healing come
>>so that we all can move on

Escape
>The rape of ebony bodies and minds
>Create the DNA to improve mankind

Break! Break! Break!
>The chains ...Escalate...Awake
>Why wait? Let the healing come*!*

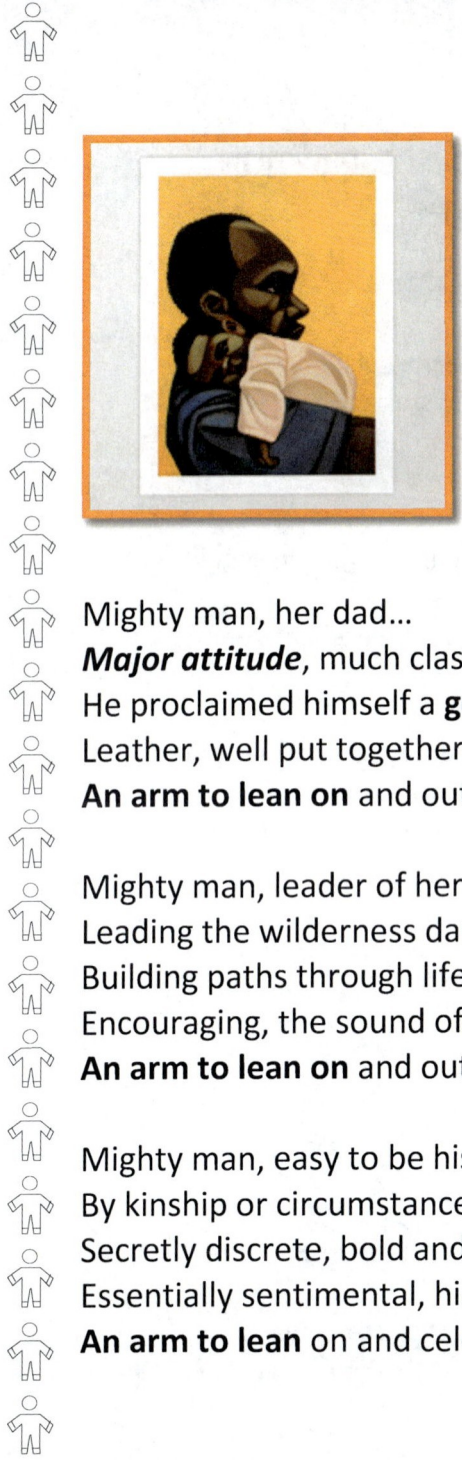

MIGHTY MAN

Mighty man, her dad...
Major attitude, much class...
He proclaimed himself a **genuine** piece of
Leather, well put together;
An arm to lean on and out-weather storms.

Mighty man, leader of her band
Leading the wilderness dance
Building paths through life's choices,
Encouraging, the sound of his voice;
An arm to lean on and out-weather storms.

Mighty man, easy to be his fan
By kinship or circumstance;
Secretly discrete, bold and strong
Essentially sentimental, his charm;
An arm to lean on and celebrate through storms...
         Mighty man*!*

MR. FINE

Scoring high strokes
Powerfully opening doors
Makin the good times roll
Obediently respecting your role

Prayer ahead of the game
Success is your aim
Earning the record you claim
Competence is your fame

Looking so divine
YOU are one-of-a-kind
When was the most recent time
You saw yourself up close, **Mr. Fine?**

Secure on your piece of the rock
Role model on your block
Incredible in your spot at the top
Your time is right, right now*!*

Esteemed and redeemed
Divine Mr. Fine

NEW POSITION

In new position
He aspires to top levels, excels, to conquest,
Acquires reputation for being his best;

In new position
Transitions into high esteem, crème-de-la-crème
Under management of authority supreme;

In new position
Seeking not his own fame, but staking claim
On *progress* in the King's name!

In position
Reaching with talent to impart
Gifts of service unto the Lord.

...Look not on his countenance, or on the height of his stature;
...for the LORD seeth not as man seeth; for man looketh on the
outward appearance, but the LORD looketh on the heart.
1 Samuel 16:23

NOTHING BETWEEN

Supportive husband
Leading *man*
Appreciative of her grand status
Prominent in her success plan

Supportive husband
True friend
He assures his star- talented wo-*man*
That upon him she can depend

With naught between
Them and their queens
But the ALMIGHTY King...

...Setting examples: how nothing is greater
Than the joy they share
With their supreme creator;
Blessed with naught less
Than sweet bonds of togetherness

PERMISSION Assigned

With big authority

He does his thing, teaching
Joy and blessedness in the songs he sings.

With big authority

Through the wilderness
He moves in a righteous groove,
    A humble attitude,
        Progressively cool.

PHILOSOPHER

Our youth must handle life right,
Clean fun must be their delight,
Focused on a joy-filled run,
Young faces smiling at the sun*!*

Wise children must be the leaders.
Can only good ones be achievers?
If you don't know I don't know either,
If they don't win we won't either*!*

"Lacks in learning
Is harmful disarmament...
Disinterest in literacy
Is dumb, plain dumb."

Society reveals
How low esteem kills
The will and makes some **brains** act ill;
Hip-hoppin through plight
Or fights **won't** decide wrong is right.
IDEAL MEN, let's lead them to project *profound* Respect*!*
May God's kingdom come;
His will for our wisdom be done.

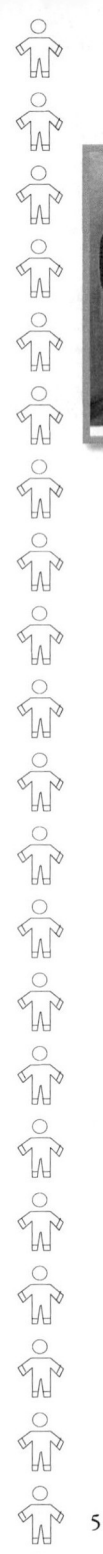

PLEDGE

(Based on Rights of Passage)

I pledge to
Appreciate my unique gifts;
Adapt positive thinking for actions that uplift;
Honor values that bring me respect;
Empower myself and excel in intellect;
Take care to project self-esteem;
Plan, expect, believe I will achieve my dreams;
Not blame others for my problems,
But face out, listen up to resolve them;
Show mature control and not angry reactions;
Lead, not seek approval nor peer satisfaction;
Live proud of who I am and can become thru Faith;
Thank my Creator everyday
For opportunities to succeed along my way;
Be led by truth guiding my adulthood.
For this is the W.O.R.D.   And it is good
(**W**isdom **O**f **R**ight **D**ecisions)

POSITIONED in Free Submission

Perseverance is his name
Endurance, his claim to fame.
May not want to, but yet he will
Do all that he must, then chill.

Bravely swallows bitter pills,
Hurt him, look out, he may forgive!
May step up by stepping back,
And react with an "intelligence" attack!

He somehow knows just what to do or say
When trouble erupts in instant replay.
Got big feet, wears suits of armor
But can be a sweetheart and charmer.

Not stuck in hate stuff, folks find him kind.
Shares daily renewal with healing in mind.
Lets go, lets God make him an example,
His attitude of fortitude gives you a sample.

Stuck in your own glue? He'll give a clue
How to move beyond mistakes and make it thru.
Flourishes positively nourished
As a real man, prayerfully *purposed!*

POSITIVE ENERGY Creating SYNERGY

Option 1
Older men: teach courage, that youth be urged
In icy winds that sting, to fly new wings.

Option 2
Young men: Emerge with courage
Based on super **star** legacies of healthy choices.

Option 3
Young gents: Surge into the future
With new wings and dreams

Your great ancestral voices say Soar*!*

PRETTY SLICK

Thought he was
Pretty boy slick
But actually movin slow

Thought he was
The slickest
Which was just a trick

Found out he was about to be picked
Off the vine not allowed to climb
Up to the top where the fruit is divine,
Because his lies revealed in time
He was not an honest friend
As he tried to pretend.

Now he is
True blue
Got his ducks in a row

Now he is
The star of the show
Although still moving sorta slow.

PRIZE FIGHTER'S FOCUS

Fights happen come what may.
He has the training to professionally fight back
With the *right* spirit of how to react;
                        With freedom to forgive;
Some who don't learn the routes to peace
Fight with fists and not brains; They strike out,
And claim you're the one to blame.
                        Having no freedom to forgive;
This prize fighter does not let anger
Force him to react and attack;
He keeps his focus and stays on track,
                        For he has freedom to forgive

This prize fighter, outside of the ring
Remains a champion inside for others to see
How to win diplomatically with the King*!*
                He's got it going on and has already won!

PURPOSED to PROGRESS

Pump up the volume purposely loud
As our **youth and seniors** seek common ground*!*
Clap your hands / As they team to explore
In a changing world, how to open new doors.
      Shout out senior rap with spiritual proof
      Jam with joy 'cause he's wise and cool;
      Expose his roots learned in old-school
      Based in a legacy of pride and truth.
Pump up the volume as spiritual leaders
Learn to follow / As well as be teachers.
Pump up the volume profound with the wisdom
To use vision to make discerning decisions;
Pump up the volume to educate and situate
Boys and men into viral spaces where they
Relate*!*

RARE but FOUND
Who is he?

A man who soars with God in control...
Who is he?

A man who can release his soul
To romance the truth of circumstance
Step up front and be blunt in his stand
Achieving and being terrific as **God's MAN.**

Who is he?
Found living unbound yet in control...What is his role?
A man who can't be bought nor sold...
Enchanting because he holds
    Power of integrity and goes about gifted as **God's MAN**.
Who is he?
His resistance is supreme...Not just an ordinary being
As he moves thru the wilderness uplifting as **God's MAN**.
In smooth grooves he tunes his steps in victorious moods

    ...As he dances with winning moves*!*
        Onlookers cheer and shout HALLELU!
As he pursues success being his best as **God's MAN***!*

(dancer: Ryan Johnson)

ROYALTY FOCUS

Recalling a Cadillac memory of times
Life cruised him along on a whirlwind ride
Because into royalty he was born
He even rode out storms in vintage form

Today is his "I've arrived" day
Enjoying a bounty of promises paid
Peace he happily lives with grace
Volumes of joy keep coming his way

By birthright he stepped into a good situation
Joy and salvation with no obligation
Pulling to the curb, steps dressed to impress;
Waves with a smile, content with blessedness*!*

STAY DRESSED UP

Look at **U,** **"gentleman deluxe"**
Clothed in caring and positive stuff…
With the SAVIOR in charge!
Got *"super"* in your personality
And it fits **U** to a "T."
Stepping styled for Prosperity!
…Confident in expectations that God will;
…Qualified to testify all is possible for Him!
Must say, you're looking great!

Look at **U** helping others be blessed,
Generous co-provider of *"happiness;"*
Soon to be planning a big Celebration?
…Brightening lives with your dedication;
'Tis *inspiring* to see how trust in the Lord
Keeps a big smile in your heart.
…Confident in expectations that God will;
…Qualified to testify all is possible for Him!
Your blessedness looks great!

SUCCESS MODEL

By thought and deed rolling up his sleeves
Pushing the levers in systems,
He helps students succeed.

>By vision impressed,
>As a wise inspiring Man
>*Educating*, pursuing plans...

Standing up on his knees
Persuasively taking the lead
In his business of building opportunities.

Models how to set goals and keep going
Beyond limits, to keep soaring, soaring
Scoring, scoring, scoring
Scoring with youth whose successes are proof!

SUGAR MAN

Sugga and spice man –
Workin your choices
Precious delightful man –
Speakin your voice
Proactive, selective man –
Sharing your presence
Secret sweetner –
Portraying love's essence
Reliable provider –
Man of the hour!
Moving higher

    Sweet fine sugga man
Explicitly designed
    Majestically inclined
        Intentionally divine
            **Blowin her mind*!*

TAUGHT and TRAINED

Unlimited dimensions you're taught to pursue
So we'll celebrate achievements that will ensue;

Principles of truth and positive esteem
Shall excel you as far as the mind's eye can see;

In summary, we have sought to educate
You with a plan for your future...
Self Determination
Purpose
Creativity
Faith

THAT KIND of MAN

She says his love is
JOY making each day a better place…
Warm hugs by the fireplace…
A fond and assuring embrace,
A private space to escape the rat race;
Sweet.

She says his love is
A bounty of impeccable tastes…
Not common place;
Mellowness at an exciting pace
JOY making each day a better place…
Sweet.
She says he's just
      that kind of man…

ULTIMATE character TRAITS
love

joy

peace

longsuffering

gentleness

goodness

faith

meekness

temperance

CORE VALUES
Confidence / Conviction / Dedication / Respect / Spirituality

What's so grand about an Ultimate Man?

...Some special kind of someone!
...A man who knows
The tools to use as he perseveres
By grace and faith
Boldly revealing strength at a winning pace
Behold his awesome traits
His hands
Poised in the tasks of doing his best
His feet
Stepping to the beat of persistence
His mind
Sowing seeds to reap the harvest of brilliance…

Proceeding into excellence beyond compare
Man extraordinaire
Assured yet humble
Walking the necessary walk; Talking truthful talk
Removing blocks in midnight hours
Placing his arm around a needy shoulder
Forcing despair to move on over
Running risks…overcoming mistakes
Kickin-it hard, opening locked gates

Leader, stellar drum major
For forthcoming generations
Requiring that they acquire supreme knowledge
Stylishly, progressively polished
An action image
Greeting men of his kind
Ahead of the line
As he waits
For wisdom and vision
To dictate his decisions
    Sometimes found hanging around
    Friends upward bound
    Beyond mundane common ground
A truly brazenly upstanding
Profound

Ultimate
MAN
What? You say you
    Know a few, one or two, too?
    Lucky you!

VIRTUAL REALITY

Where he once lived
Disgraceful low tastes displaced hope and faith
But

He prayed

And prayed...And for him somebody prayed
And prayer
Led him to investigate another place
And instigate a change of pace
And restructure hope and faith in a cleaner space
Proving that prayer can do many things...like provide
The wind beneath ones wings into a new reality...

His prayers are propping open new doors
...Stepping him out of negative focus
Into sensational Revelations, where hope
Prompts him to proceed and mount up on faith...
...Takes laughter along on the ride;
A joyful beat repeats,
Releasing his feet to skip to a galloping song,
As he joins the loud crowd in the free spirit zone
Inspired!
New fire!
Moving higher!

WALKING in the VALLEY

Stumbling in the valley
Fumbling toward the goal
Been crawling down the alley
Crumbling in his soul...
Seems no one was listening,
Who cared if he would cry?
Leaning on sheer resistance
Refusing despite hard times to rely
On excuses and alibis;

Burdened down with heartache
Scorned each way he turned
Begging in a futile state
Forlorn, all bridges burned;
Mercy's blessed assistance
Came walking by his side
SHOVING him with insistence
Refueling with inside sunshine
To dry his weeping eyes.

Though he fall, he shall not be utterly cast down:
for the LORD upholdeth him with *his hand.*
Psalm 37:24

WARRIOR Dreamer Drum Major

Strategically ***armed*** for spiritual warfare,
Performed feats that would defeat lesser beings,
Excelled as an achiever, equipped as a believer;
God's **Real man.**
    Linking time, circumstance, progressive essence
    Taught us how in hope to trust;
    Competing and preaching endurance lessons;
    God's **Real man.**

Going far beyond just doing his part
With prayer that sustains strength
Using power of mind, and love in his heart;
God's **Real man.**
    Some call him a hero, with supreme traits;
    Dreaming real equality with building blocks of faith
    Extraordinary efforts, fueled by amazing grace
        As we proclaimed
        "What Manner of Man*!* is THIS!"

Watch Them Show, Tell, and Excel!

Star that rises within his heart;
Truth that dwells in his mind;
See him as a dawn that lights the way
In to higher heights
By faith beyond mere sight.

Embraced by grace;   Full of courage;
Stumble? Momentarily he may,
But strong of *will*, he sustains;
Evidence of His strength to proclaim.
     What manner of MAN is This!
Community and Christian unity on his " list"
…Concentrating not on the problems,
Demonstrating *how* to solve them;
Joining the ranks of anointed others
Opening doors for sisters and brothers;

Some instructing with pastoral wisdom and vision
*How to let **God's Will** guide our decisions*;
And some instruct youth about spiritual essence
Through examples and reverent lessons.

'Way Up in His Sky

Youth jumps with joy over a glorious possibility to Celebrate grandiose probabilities

...endowed with abilities for greatness,
...qualified and inspired on a mission to give God the glory...
Grabs opportunities to use authority from a rich Powerful Father
Who lets him know he's got it going strong...
Box back! Fight with insight if life's ring is getting tight! So recite
Some positive rap and go! and hold on! ...And come on into the
Land of Milk and Honey, **Get the race won, Party started, Job done,
Hesitation overcome! PAUSE to Praise** and shout because
the *Promise* has been signed and sealed... and *he does deliver!*

WHEN? NOW! Win!
He is of the "When" generation
Confident, courageous, obedient, Endowed!
He is blessed with a holy affirmation:
That I can and I will overcome with expedience...
WHEN? NOW!
He is given a promise to receive
From an omnipotent omnipresent master, the passion
For living a life filled trust and belief
With joy, rewarding his spirit with lasting satisfaction
Positioned to name it, he speaks it, claims it,
Moving assuredly happily blessed
By grace
Over-ruling opinions that may cite his mistakes;
Dancing through the Wilderness
With faith
He says, it's definite, baby, not a mere "maybe"
That He'll never leave nor forsake me!

When She Whines

Progressively timed, he gives inspiring advice
    To think first, then decide what's right;
    A real friend of who listens with attention
    When she whines…

His words of cheer remind her he's near
    Saying, " Focus, my dear, get it clear;"
    Stressing encouragement she needs to hear…

His smooth moves
    Help put things back on track
    Saying, "Honey, tighten up your act,"
    When she whines…

His patient pace when she makes hasty mistakes
    He reminds her, "Darling, wait;"
    Then helps her get it straight…

His needed push is an on-time gift,
    A perfect uplift
    When plans go adrift…
    And she just wishes and whines…

    He speaks truth,   not hype,
    With power that invites joy into life,
    Providing awesome displays of faith and insight,
    That even without words can rhyme…

WHO is HE? Power in the Crowd!

We know him as a track burner.
He shows he is consistent and committed;
Goal seeker minute by minute,
Knowing he's gonna be a front runner
Insured with what it takes to win…

We know him as a ruling man with a plan.
He explores to gain all the knowledge he can;
Envisioning changes he can command,
Profound power clasped in his hands…
Insured with what it takes to win!

Willing Winning Wise = Wonderful

wise

upright

cooperative *reliable*

temperate *kind*

humble *honorable*

WINNING WARS with PEACE

He's his brother's keeper
A determined teacher and leader
Teaching positive cooperative attitudes
And togetherness are the winning tools.

His **focus** and direction
His **strength** and protection
His armor sword and shield
Make his enemies yield.

Admitting, Lord, I can't,
But I know, I *know* , *I know* YOU can…
Step into youthful minds, make love the plan…

Direct the route
As they take their brothers' hands.

WISELY ABIDING

How is it that
> In the midst of difficulty one can still be glad?

Through life's strife and confusion
> God still commands?

It is *what it is*:
> He is a Warrior blessed and assured...
> A contender whose agenda of righteousness rules;
> A Kingdom mindset dictates his decisions.
> In sync with his faith, God makes provisions;
> When all is not well and trouble prevails

A king sized shoulder and mighty hand
Help him carry out plans
> In the space where he stands
>> and works as God's man;
>
> Not perfect, perhaps with
>> a thorn in his side,
>
> Obedient and forgiven,
>> with joy he abides.
>
> He knows to hold on;
>> an Ambassador to the throne,

A blessed and assured MAN!

Words Smiling at Ultimate MEN

Loving you, real men who treat others
Like stars in God's parade; who project respect
And are deeply ingrained with the spirit to teach
Youth what it takes to thrive and reach dreams.

Loving you, real men who delight
In honoring the right of women to be treated sweetly
Respecting them completely, knowing to discretely
Love a real wo-man...Like a real man*!*

When you real men go strolling by we'll grin
        Because we'll be feeling so proud...
When you mighty men contend we'll blush
        Because we'll be oh so touched...
When you come walking in we'll smile (out loud)
        Because we be liking your style...
We'll glow as our pleasure shows*!*

WORKIN' IT WITH HIM

Most folks would say It is so fun,
Like dipping friendly toes
In the flow of a healing stream;
Take it from those who know
A friendship of sharing dreams,
Working with a man of God.

Most folks would say It is so easy,
Planting tiny talent seeds
And gardens for kids' esteem
On the roads to their victories;
Workin' with him is astonishing,

Working with a man of God...*Agree?*

YES, HE is ALL THAT, *ALL That!*

Notice
>You'll see
>How he
>>Arrives in transformation
>>By kingly proclamation;

Applaud
>As he
>Diligently
>>Creates pace for 1st place,
>>Moves ahead with faith;

Say Yea
>When he
>Leads others
>>Displaying plans to win;
>>Born: great among men*!*

YOU KNOW WHAT?

Not by accident, we've discovered
Paths to progress through one another;
We are winning the race
As a generation putting love in first place!
Love for each other is our objective,
A prized goal we have selected.
Let peace be the winner, victoriously enacted
As the future for families is securely erected.

**Ultimate men are spiritually akin
In covenant as brothers,**
        Answers to discover;
              Hand in hand hearts in accord
Enacting plans of what thus says the Lord.

**It is just that simplistic...
Ultimate men are significantly
Terrific** !

You're STEPPIN

You step up to the plate
At a winner's gait, a rapid pace.
A mighty man doing all you can
To live in the promised land
Of today, doing your best
To enjoy success!

    You hear the ladies sigh
    To the thrill of you passing by;
    Oh, look at that marvelous guy!

    They blush and try
    To get your eye;
    But you're busy steppin!

A lady hunches her friend,
"Watch him achieving his dreams."
Say what they wanna
You ain't gonna
Let anything stand in your way.
Got a calling you must obey.

Obviously, you've made a decision
To model in example as young boys transition
Into Ultimate Manhood!

YOU'VE SURFACED in Love

Beneath the surface is where we longed to meet
As bubbles of anticipation rose up from our hearts;
There trust resides and pretense does not abide
And desire gives caution the freedom to step aside,
And just be us.

Beneath the surface joy is loosed to sing
And hope dances through wilderness and flings
Away shyness and blushes to express blessedness,
As we laugh at our silliness,
And just be us.

Beneath the surface we've allowed the seed
Of love to spring up and bloom as we see
What divineness looks like, sharing with delight,
Secret reasons in a new season to laugh in smiles;
And just be us.

YOUR
JAZZY
JASS

Rhythm that swoons
    With a rapturous tune
        Filling life's rooms
            With sweet scented blooms

Sunshine of life
    Evoking delight strokin truth
        Provokin winnin moods
            Deep in our minds

It romances the atmosphere
    Your jass
        It enhances the environment
            With your class

Inspiring rhapsodies poetically
    Flowing, edifying mankind's being
        Boldly alluring, reassuring
            Progressive melodies

Your classy
    Jazzy
        jass

ZONE: Business/Community/Country

A wealth of knowledge gives him power to excell.
Beyond the call of duty his skill serves us well.
What a spirit of conserving and preserving he embraces.

A resource,
Connecting, correcting, directing, protecting
Excelling in the contributions he makes.

We appreciate w*ho and whose* he is as he provides
Assistance, convenience, services, and supplies.

ZONE: Family and Home

Protective fathers bravely stand and say
      Be sure to treat their children the right way
      Plus the <u>Ultimate Man</u> won't take no stuff
      If you mistreat or treat his kids too rough;
See, he fits God's definition: Gentle *but* tough.

A caring father figure teaches "aim high;"
      He's a real man upon whom kids can rely
      About pride and respect, there's no "maybe"
      By example he proves truth then *restates* it
He fits God's intervention: Direct *or* persuasive.

God's man does not always reside in the sky
      In our hearts he's there perhaps quite alive
      He mightily watches over the treasured fold
      And to him we are more precious than gold.
He fits God's plan: Prayer is strength for his role.

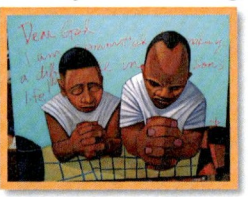

ZONE: Teaching Hope and Victory

He teaches: **Positive energy of Hope with Faith
Connects us to victory and truth of God's grace.**
> *Shelter in my shadow / refuge in my fortress
> Love is the protection one receives if one believes.*

He teaches: **Divine synergy, a combined reprieve
That embraces the promise made on Calvary.**
> *My yoke is easy, trust and believe
> No matter the problem, I'll set you free.*

He teaches: **Blessedness is power, supreme**
Bringing joy to mankind's hopes and dreams.
Birthed out of burden; reborn unto me
No matter the problem, I'll set you free.

Distressed by *Neucrotical,* **deadly disbelief?**
Obsessed? Depressed? What can't you believe?
Let's stretch your mind, so you will see
Promises thru faith's new possibilities.

He teaches **self esteem and worth…**
Man: body out of dirt ; Soul: spiritual birth
Wo-man: formed from man; Purpose: God's work.
He teaches: *Know the truth – be set free.*
His message has that authority;
His honor is deliverance unto God's creation
Knowledge of obedience to our Rock of salvation!

91

ZONE: Where Pride Resides

Honorable men
Make noble decisions
To stand tall and observe family traditions;
To boldly uphold and enforce family pride
To build esteem and make dreams come alive.
In families with plenty, and families with few
The paths of their footsteps have led us through,
On into celebrations where we victoriously dance
As the family of
MAN
Through the Wilderness*!*

ZONE: Dance Class

She asked, "Can I pick my music next time?
  I like music better that rhymes."
He said, "That's not always how life is designed."
  Then assured her that she was learning fine.
As you grow you'll learn to rewind,
Adjust
When you must,
Refocus
Change your motions,
Remove
What refuses to improve,

And tune your heart to the beat of joyous sunshine.
That's how a good life is designed.

ZONE: THE ROUTE OUT

In a ONENESS spirit onto the streets they came
    Nearly 20 thousand strong **real men** to claim
Their status as men with the urgent message
    To ***stop the violence*** and project love's essence
With a stand for peace in a togetherness presence

Hope thundered through streets on a dreamship ride
    Brothers marching with pride by the preacher's side…
Parting the sea of indifference as only they could
    Despite possible harm, giving hope to the neighborhood
With a stand for peace in a togetherness presence

The crowd shouted encouraging brave brothers
    Contending for faith showing support for each other
On a righteous path to help align for all mankind
    A freedom from WAR time frame of mind
And break the chain of kin-against-kin crime

A march for peace defending our right to escape
    Our self-inflicted hate and navigate
A start toward stepping up to investigate
    How to perpetrate **love instead of hate**,
And change the signs of perilous times*!*

                        Dedicated to Pastor Dr. F. Clark
                        From *Dancing Through the Wilderness*

ZONE: Training Space

...endowed with abilities for greatness,
...qualified and inspired on a mission to
Reach the highest height,
He boxes back! Fights with insight!
Recites something positive!
Gets the study session started, Job done,
Hesitation overcome!
PAUSES to consider solutions
Before jumping to conclusions...
Recites something positive!
Is observed sharing
Compassionate caring;
Investigates and creates!
Maps out plans to do the best he can!
Learning to become a real man!

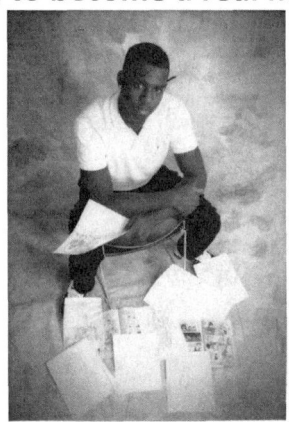

ZONE: MAN hood

He is God's MAN purposed and designed
      In agreement with the plan
           Creation has in mind
To fulfill his role in the family fold
      To help achieve dreams
           Find means to mend fragile seams.
He is the salt seasoning family courage
      Based in faith...
           Building a legacy as they flourish.
His goals blend connecting, reflecting, expecting.
Calmed by motion of the skies, air, waters
He is assured by the reigning sameness.

He is thankful for anchors...
By himself but not alone
      In the Master's comfort zone...
What manner of MAN is he!
Soul luxuriating as *God's Man* in victory*!*